A Book Of Poems

Joseph Hart

ISBN: 978-93-6354-504-5

First Edition: 2024
Rs. 200/-

Cyberwit.net
HIG 45 Kaushambi Kunj, Kalindipuram
Allahabad - 211011 (U.P.) India
http://www.cyberwit.net
Tel: +(91) 9415091004
E-mail: info@cyberwit.net

Christians and republicans have an insatiable interest in – and a lot of opinions about – other people's sex life.

Tell me, Mr. Congressman, when you're having a chat with God, do the two of you talk about anything but yourself and your goodness?

America was not meant to be a Christian country.
It's a country where people are free to be Christian.

The world's greatest works of imagination
are not its art, but its religions.

If Israel weren't Jewish, would you still like
what it's doing to the people in Gaza?

Contents

Maxx

Like playing dice for the robe of Christ!
This is how it seems
To publish songs about the death
Of the sweetest of my dreams.

My little cat died long ago.
The memory is gold.
The only thing in nature -
Just love does not get old.

Maxx & Piso

I loved you very much.
Now that you are gone
I see I must forget you
Just to carry on.

Truth? If there's a Truth
It's one I never knew.
You loved music. You had treasures.
Yet you are dying too.

Ritual

Wake in the morning
And wash your face,
Then devoutly pray
At 7 -
To guarantee
That there's a place
For your plump little bigoted
Body in heaven -

Lines

When little Fred goes
I'm going too.
Is there a heaven?
The sky isn't blue.

Is anything right?
Is anything true?
Is there a heaven?
I haven't a clue.

Ayn Rand

Miracles (technology) -
Biographies of men
Written – all with selfless
Anonymity -
Castles and cathedrals,
Monuments of stone
All which seem impossible
To be built at all -
By authors and inventors
Now forgotten,
Never known -
Wonders of the world
That integrity has made -
Demolished in a flicker
By tiny selfish minds
That couldn't for a minute
Have done what has been done -

Not All

Some animals are butchers,
Just like people.
Not all. And some republicans
Are sane and decent people.
Some cops are brave and gentle.
Some therapists are kind.
Some Christians are not bigots.
Not all of them. Not all of them.
Not all of them.

The Crow

I saw a crow just eat a little food
Left out for the cats. Then turn around
And drink a little water from a bowl,
Then turn around and eat a little more,
Then turn again and take another sip -
Then flap his giant wings and fly away.
A treasure just to watch! How did he know
The dish held food
Or that the bowl held water?

Lines

Ziggurats and pyramids -
Safe from the unknown -
They fortify their nonsense
With cathedrals made of stone.

Rituals and feathers -
The wise forever knew
With so much gold and ceremony
Surely it is true.

David

“Now at last I’m strong,”
Little David said;
“And what I was thinking
Is clear inside my head.”
Then he went to tell them.
But age got there instead.
When he arrived he found
That all of them were dead.

Maxx

Maxx lay sleeping on my lap.
I looked down and saw
A thing I'd never seen before;
But I recognized it.

This little beast feels love for me,
A feeling in his body.
He purrs when he is petted; often
Comes when he is called.

For Edna Millay

Talent isn't learned.
It's just the way you are.
From the brow of Gods
It springs full-grown.
All the stones in Christendom
Do not make a star.
A light is born in some,
The way is shown.

Mini

Where does Mini poop?
Where does Mini poop?
On the grass or in the garden?
A little vagrant cat!

A stray – from the beginning
Eager to be touched -
She sleeps outside the door
Or sits looking through the glass.

There's a bowl of water
And a little dish of food
On the concrete. And she's happy
To be petted while she eats.

Status

A Nobel prize for Dylan -
The presidency for Trump -
A Pulitzer for Sondheim -

Homicide in Gaza
And murders in Ukraine -
The world was seldom sensible.
Now it is insane!

Lines

The suicide lay dying
And with his final breath
He said, “Some things are even
Worse than death.”

Culture

Americans take selfies -
Laugh at universities -
Give themselves a high five -
And think Monet's a beer.

Lines

Momma, momma,
When will I die?
Will it be soon?
Will it be soon?
Is there anything
In the sky -
Maybe a heaven
Behind the moon?

The Stray Cat

Was there ever a cat
Who so liked to be petted -
Around your legs
Or in a chair?
When you start to walk away,
He's there.

He shares the water.
He shares the food.
Nothing is really his.
He'll nip your finger
Or bite your foot.
If this isn't love,
What is?

Him

He preferred a philistine life
Of promiscuity and love
(Wisdom in a can of beer
And a cigarette)
Than to walk around
And think great thoughts.

Horror, Pain

Morals and convictions
That would dim a star -
Homophobes and racists -
What monsters Christians are!

Thinking that they know
What no one ever knew -
Are there gentle Christians?
Yes, but just a few -

A Thought

Dinosaurs and cats
Needn’t to rehearse
Their spontaneity
(Or affection – which is worse)
Nor wonder when they dream:
“What’s not the universe?”

An Ugly Poem

"Will they blow up the world today?
Tell me, mother, do."
In spite of his silliness and conceit,
If he hadn't been a genius
Keats would be forgotten too.
Disinterred, a corpse decays in heat.

Lines

Are Larry Hart and Keats
The only loves I ever had?
Looking at my poetry, I think,
"The ideas may be good,
But the songs are bad."
Even music into nothingness
Will sink.

Immigrants

Eight years ago
Children at the border
Were put in cages.
Now it's going to be
Taking millions from their homes.
Bigots always lose.
How many people died before they did?
Oh Jesus Christ!
Is there no hell for Trump?

"Battle Hymn Of The Republic"

(after Julia Ward Howe)

Mine eyes have seen the glory of
The coming of the Lord.
If you have a couple billion
And you feel a little bored
America's a country you can
Easily afford.
The Truth is up to you.

In the beauty of the lilies Christ was
Born across the sea.
You can lock up little children.
You can alter history.
The supremacists will love you. You'll have
Immortality.
And God is on your side.

Oh! "You can grab a pussy."
Global warming isn't real.
Mexicans and immigrants
Are underneath your heel.
Like Jesus you'll be persecuted.
Animals don't feel.
When you are a star!

You'll feel mighty as an eagle with
Your woman standing there.
She will be an angel to all
Children blond and fair.
As for dark complected ones, she
"Really doesn't care."
Porn stars cost you dear!

Mock the weak, your fans will
Imitate the things you do.
Coin a phrase too infantile for
People over two.
Watch the children die and claim
It's not because of you.
You did nothing wrong.

The Christians call you holy. You're a
Saint among your kin.
You gave an extra meaning to
The noble thought of sin.
More popular than Jesus! You're
A little God of Tin.
A prophecy come true!

Standing like a Titan
And indifferent to tears,
A brain without an equal
And a penis with no peers;
Never mind the children.
You'll be President for years.
Iran don't frighten you.

The Constitution's history but
Meaningless today.
Science is ridiculous and
Reason is passe.
Bigots made you President and
They are here to stay.
God bless the USA!

Notre Dame

Notre Dame's
Gone up in flames
And the fat American liar
Belches twice
And tweets advice
To the people fighting the fire.

Trump's America

Who thought that I was capable
Of such enormous rage
And hatred as I feel for Donald Trump?
A man without the smallest trace
Of conscience or compassion
Or intelligence -
And ridiculous!
Who could love that man?
But millions do.
America is not the country
(Or it never was)
It hollers to the planet that it is.

My Grandmother

I went to see her daily.
She liked vanilla milk shakes.
The ebb of her intelligence.
I never told my Grandmother
I loved her.

MAGA

"Make America Great Again"
Backward we shall go
To the days of Joe McCarthy,
The evil of Jim Crow,
Keeping gays in closets
And women's status low.

A Tragedy

The farmer left his house
With a mallet and a gun.
"I'm going to kill that dog," he thought;
"And it will be fun."

The little boy just watched.
It was an easy kill.
He didn't do a thing,
And God was very still.

No one saw it happen.
He thought,"I wasn't brave.
I betrayed his trust.
And now he's in a grave."

The days continued on,
Though nothing lay ahead.
"I let him kill my dog,"
Was all he ever said.

Cats

Cats don't blink their eyes.
Never, never, never.
They're crazy or they're wise,
Simple or they're clever.

They roll around the floor.
Tell me, little pet:
Is death an open door?
It hasn't happened yet.

Lines

With books and music -
I never wanted to be loved -
Except maybe by the cats.
What is a kiss for?
It doesn't feel like anything.
I've never felt lonely;
Bored perhaps, but not lonely.
Maybe these things are better -
Just a little boring.
I don't give you pain
And I don't give you love.
Maybe not giving you love
Causes you pain.

Life

I brutalized Jay and Gary.
The rest? I just went away.
Madness destroys! And life
Is over in a day.

Can this be a poem? It's not
What they are writing now.
Talent and rhythm and music -
Maybe they don't know how.

Thousands and thousands of poets -
The gate is open wide
And countless poets rush through it
In a ceaseless tide.

Rhythm and rhyme are forgotten.
These poets never doubt
They're brilliant. But given the form -
What to write poems about?

While Petting Fred

Animals just live
And do not question why -
Just dirt beneath their feet
And only planets in the sky.
People – who are selfish -
Think animals don't cry.
I wonder whether animals
Know they're going to die.

History

History children
Aren't taught in school:
Created by racists,
Destroyed by a fool.

Do these lovers of Trump
(How their halos glisten!)
Believe what they say,
Or even listen?

Innocent immigrants -
The Christian's prey -
Are slandered, uprooted
And driven away.

The Reprieve

I have a photo of myself
At 8 or 9 or 10
Standing by my Grandpa,
My arm around his shoulder,
And his arm around my waist.
On my face: a smirk.
A childish smirk.
My father saw the photo
And he sneered.
He sneered at me. I'm sure
I know what he was thinking.
He hated he, it never stopped.
Such evil in a child!
My Grandpa was his father.
Today – at last today -
I saw it! I just saw it!
A picture of a boy
About the age that I was then.
While his mother held him -
Dear Jesus! - in the picture
The little boy was smirking.
I knew it – or I hoped -
It was just a childish thing.

The Animals

The cruelty of people!
They kill the animals
For pleasure and for food
And for expensive furs,
And for many thousand years,
For favors from their Gods,
Gods they think prefer them
To the animals.
And most ridiculous -
The Christians go one better:
Every creature on the earth
Was made to please the people -
Like dinosaurs and fleas.

Convinced

Here is a bigot.
Here is a thief.
Nothing they do retards
Their love of Trump
Or unquestioned belief
That heaven is in the cards.

Crazy

Can you drive a person crazy?
Yes, you can.
Especially a very
Baffled man
Who makes a mess of
Everything that is,
But can't demand what is
Already his.
In a world where
Everyone is strong,
The frightened and the weak
Do not belong.

Age

Animals stay beautiful
After they are old -
Then they go away
And die alone.

People just get ugly –
Monsters of decay,
Unloveable -
Except by little children.

Lines

I loved him forever.
He loved me a day.
Fetch up a casket
To take me away,
A heartless cadaver,
A corpse with no soul,
And off through the rain
Let the little cart roll
That carries my body
With nothing inside,
Gone like a wave
That goes out with the tide.
Over the cobblestones,
Roughly I'll ride,
And no one will know
Or remember I died.
There on the bed
Of a small wooden cart,
Take my cadaver
That hasn't a heart.
Plod an old horse
Through the miserable rain
Down to the graveyard
Where nothing feels pain.
I perished for love,
And I perished in vain,
Bones and a body
And organs and brain,
But never a heart.

No, never again!
Deep, deep in a hole
Shall my body remain
Til worms have devoured it.
I am insane.

The Tavern

On the chalice,
Old and fine,
Proust is the patina.
And the sign
In front of the tavern
Is seldom seen.
Mozart is heaven.
Keats is the wine;
Rodgers & Hart divine.
Meursault is the consort,
Murdoch the queen.
I drink alone,
And the tavern is mine.

An Epigram

When hopes and fears have been dispersed,
I have two cats and music. Cursed
Am I. Of all bad men, the worst.
I never said "I love you" first.

Cats

When a cat's in trouble,
It's his lot
To cry until he's rescued,
Or he's not.

Cats

Do cats like wicked people?
They sleep beside the old -
And were once entombed with kings
In pyramids of gold.

The Misunderstanding

He brought flowers to the house,
Dried ones. I liked him.
I was uncomfortable, I said nothing.
I was afraid of saying something gauche.
Finally he said,
"I'll go find someone who wants to talk to me!"
And he left, and I was happy
Because it meant he'd wanted to talk to me.
And he never understood
Why I hadn't talked to him,
And he never knew that I liked him.

Music

Music lasts forever,
Composers not as long.
Cziffra makes a heaven
Where the Gods belong.
While I hug my cat,
I say nothing wrong.

Music is eternal.
Just musicians die.
There's nothing except stars
And planets in the sky.
Do animals and cats
Know they're going to die?

Freddy's Song

Hello, my Freddy.
Hello, my kitty.
Hello, my little black cat.
Freddy, you're where it's at.
Now what do you think of that?

Looking At Maxx

An injured or a burping cat
Looks into the distance,
Like an infant child who doesn't
Know what's going on.

Death

Cats – why must they die -
Like the gentle cats who loved me?
Or Gershwin, Chopin – both
Dead at 39?

The cat lies on my lap.
I think - “Why must he die?”
As I think it has been thought
Since a million years ago.

Old

Shriveled, wrinkled and flabby,
Loved only by my tabby -
I look in a mirror and see
A thing that can't really be me.

In spite of what youth intends,
This is how it ends.
But genius made Horowitz sing,
And his age was a beautiful thing.

Love

A cat who is crippled or scalded,
Maybe lost most of his fur,
Still wants to be cuddled and petted,
And still when he's happy will purr.

Alone in a wilderness crying,
Caught with compassion and care
By someone who's very much kinder
Than Jesus, who wasn't there.

Love

Love – the kindest of all accidents -
In imagination where is wrought
The infinite variety of sense -
Is created out of nothing – like a thought.

Let me live in a palace all my own
As far from men as now from yesterday -
Pretend I'm not and never was alone.
Love's something to believe in, anyway.

Maxx

I'm different from my cat
And he is different from me.
It's happiness and love that give us
Similarity.

He sleeps across my arm.
I like to hear him purr.
Both of us will die
As if we never were.

My Grandfather

Enclosing, warm and strong,
He saw nothing wrong
In me. He went away.
I'm alone today.
Tall and never old,
Never cross or cold,
Whom no one will replace.
I can hear his voice
And I can see his face.
His unerring hand
Would set a sparrow free.
Compassionate and gentle -
At least he was with me.

Lines

An endless number of people
For thousands and thousands of years -
Some of them composers -
Even beauty disappears.

Cats and dogs who loved them -
All of them lost somehow -
Even their graves forgotten -
Where is beauty now?

Death

If there's a heaven,
Let it be
For books, the cats,
My Grandpa and me
And music.
God is no
Necessity.
I'm going away.
I'm going away.
Beyond the sky,
Beyond the sea.

Bugs

They're frightened and they run.
They do not want to die.
Crushed to death by people
Who see Jesus in the sky -
Men who think some God
Made the world for just a few
People who kill other people too.

Perfect Perfect People

I don't like perfect people!
People who know how
To talk to other people
With perfect savoir faire,
Emotionally perfect,
Gauging every comment
To make the right impression
And have the right effect.
They know themselves completely
And understand the heart.
Are such people happier
Than clumsy men like me?

In The Times

A thousand bombed out houses
In Gaza and Ukraine -
Searching through the rubble
To find what may remain -
In exactly like my home -
Somehow yet to fall
Is a single picture hanging
On a single standing wall -

Pagans

Sitting in the winter
In the silence of my flat
Contemplating pagans
While I hold my sleeping cat -
The aim of Christ – the Christians really
Made a mess of that.
All the ancient deities
Are old and rather worn.
From the womb of heresy
Will other Gods be born?

Unwound

In anticipation
Or the throes of an attack,
He played a foolish ass,
Instead of fighting back.

If only at the first
(Strange though it may seem),
Many people loved him.
Madness is a dream.

Lines

Animals love.
It’s as simple as that.
I never knew
A bigoted cat.

They don’t shoot guns.
They are not cursed
With hells. Or yell,
“My country first!”

Do cats go to heaven
Or only die?
If they don’t go to heaven,
Neither will I.

Love without God -
A wish and a star -
God without love -
That's how things are -

For Oscar Wilde

Dig among the garbage.
If it's holy you will find
A hundred Christian bigots.
Is there any other kind?

People who are moral
Make their goodness known.
And underneath their shirt
Beats a heart of stone.

For Dory Previn

The rhesus monkey and the cloth mother -
The boy and his teddy bear -
The paper describing Jesus
Tossed into the garbage by mistake
So there is no Jesus anywhere or ever -
Is heaven true
Or do I just want it to be?

For Robin

A soft little doggy
All fluffy and white
Sat by a river
And all though the night
He barked at the shadows,
He barked at the cars,
He barked at the river,
He barked at the stars.
He barked and he barked.
Why, this loud little pup
Even barked at the people
His barking woke up.

Pieta

When crazy Jesus
Was nailed to a cross,
Mary, his mother, mourned.
Dead he lay across her lap.
To her he wasn't a God;
He was her son.

Sweet Fantasy

My God is a Sunday School Jesus
Surrounded by children
And holding a lamb -
Neither a racist nor homophobe -
Ugly words that should not be
In a song about my God.

www.ingramcontent.com/pod-product-compliance
Ingram Content Group UK Ltd.
Pitfield, Milton Keynes, MK11 3LW, UK
UKHW041316190726
13845UKWH00025B/297